Summertime RHYMES

Sizzling Sensations

Edited By Donna Samworth

First published in Great Britain in 2016 by:

YoungWriters

Coltsfoot Drive
Peterborough
PE2 9BF
Telephone: 01733 890066
Website: www.youngwriters.co.uk

Book Design by Jenni Harrison

SB ISBN 978-1-78624-609-7
Printed and bound in the UK by BookPrintingUK
Website: www.bookprintinguk.com
YB0291J

Foreword

Welcome, Reader!

For Young Writers' latest competition, *Summertime Rhymes*, we gave young poets nationwide the task of writing a poem all about summer, and they rose to the challenge magnificently!

Our aspiring poets have also developed their creative skills along the way, getting to grips with poetic techniques such as rhyme, simile and alliteration to bring their thoughts to life. The result is this entertaining collection that evokes the fun of summer and summons the sunshine whatever the time of year.

Here at Young Writers our aim is to encourage creativity in children and to inspire a love of the written word, so it's great to get such an amazing response, with some absolutely fantastic poems.

I'd like to congratulate all the young authors in this anthology, and I hope this inspires them to continue with their creative writing.

Contents

Independent Entries

Elizabete Ivanova (8) 1
Lola Mujungu (8) 2
Ella Paterson (9) 4
Rhianna Sunassee (9) 6
Leah Young (10) 8
Max Lishman-Neilson (10) 9
Alisha Ghogha (10) 10
Michael Sirapob Brown (9) 11
Sneha Bhudia (10) 12
Heidi Hanson 13
Keziah Davies (10) 14
Aimee Hood (10) 15
Bhavika Mistry (9) 16
Hanuv Garg (9) 18
Jamie Thomas Kitchen 20
Rutendo Muchechesi (9) 22
Lila Roberts (9) 23
Ini Atinaro (10) 24
Anjal Parizad (9) 26
Eloise C E Matthews (6) 27
Gavyam Garg (7) 28
Emily Ann Thomas (8) 29
Serena Oduka (9) 30
Anika Jain (8) 31
Ryan Laurent Xavier Ssimbwa (7) 32
Tee-Jay Bruce (10) 33
Shreelakshmi Raghuvaran (8) 34
Sadiman Khan (13) 35
Ella Schofield (10) 36
Ria Elizabeth Sanderson (8) 37
Glory Nwangwu (9) 38
Mya Khela (7) 39
Maryam Asghar (9) 40
Lisette G J Matthews (5) 41
Kayla Freeman (9) 42
Emilija Atkins (10) 44
Emmanuela Opara (7) 45
Isabella Barber (9) 46
Emma Mahata (6) 47
Charlee Elizabeth Wilson (8) 48
Amiee Cox (10) 49
Vedika Sandeep (10) 50
Maariyah Daud (10) 52
Ema Bredova (10) 54
Favour Joy Olorunfemi (8) 56
Lucy Mackie (10) 58
Lina Sahal (10) 59
Nuala Sankey (9) 60
Jasmine Richards (10) 61
Jahanavee Sandeep (8) 62
Zain Jamil (9) 63
Olivia Howell (11) 64
Harriet Tracey (10) 65
Sarah Faraz (10) 66
Vishaagan Vanigasooriar (8) 67
Gabriela Kalinowska (8) 68
Sithija Kurukulasuriya (5) 69
Michelle Oreoluwa Alalade (6) 70
Yusairah Syed (9) 71
Emily Chambers (7) 72
Beatrice Isted-Aggrey (8) 73
Jack Freeman (8) 74
Faith Schooley (12) 75
Rachael Ruixi Chen (8) 76
Toyin Sarah Joseph (10) 77
Jayden Roberts (10) 78
Zara Zeynal (9) 79
Syed Ali Tahir (10) 80

Amoya Mullings (9) 81
Alima Khanum (12) 82
Tarneen Kaur Gura (9) 83
Eva Smith (6) 84
Jasmeen Kaur Gura (10) 85
Charlotte Rose Heppenstall (8) 86
Joshua Skidmore (9) 87
Humairah Banu Akhter (6) 88
Skye Jessie Hill (9) 89
Aasiyah Shajira (9) 90
Chijioke Nathaniel Ibeanu (8) 91
Paula Ampaw-Obeng (10) 92
Hafsah Mahmood (9) 93
Lexie Witcher (8) 94
Poppy Bradford (9) 95
Swasthika Arunkumar (10) 96
Ella Plumb (10) 97
Imogen Lewis (7) 98
Anusha Shams (8) 99
Amalya-Lovett Akua Antwi-Agyei (9) 100
Klyo Anerobi-Mcpherson (8) 101
Ocean Tallulah Walton (10) 102
Paris Kia Cookson (10) 103
Dana Farajallah (9) 104
Megha Sheby (9) 105
Harriet Rose Kemeny (10) 106
Paul Beard (8) 107
Poppy Reeves (10) 108
Umar Francesco Kunateh (6) 109
Aleš Kilpatrick (7) 110
Aamna Begum (6) 111
Matthew Munson (8) 112
Madison Keiley Elliott (9) 113
Honey Edwards (7) 114
Aleema Mirza Hamid (9) 115
Isabel Amelia Arrowsmith (10) 116
Keira Ureta (7) 117
Layla Zewin (7) 118
Zara Ahmad (8) 119
Ross Jefferies (9) 120
Jitong Yi (11) 121
Hadiyh Roostaei (10) 122
Kerensa Meredith Lawrence (6) 123
Raihan Rahman 124
Aubrey Walton (8) 125
Luca Scanlon (7) 126
Misba Khan (9) 127
Pola Szczygielek (6) 128
Umaima Ayaz (9) 129
Ovidiu Baraban (8) 130
Luca Nocerino (7) 131
Hamza Ahmad (11) 132
Rishabh Murali (8) 133
Annabel Lucy Bulley (8) 134
Hannah Thomas (7) 135
Charlotte Barber (7) 136
Alice Emily Bradley (5) 137
Harry Munson (6) 138
Emily Walker (9) 139
Tyra Sackey (8) 140
Jenny Yule (9) 141
Harshant Singh Randhawa (7) 142
Ty McCann (10) 143
Isabelle Wooldridge (6) 144
Emma Hollie Birch (7) 145
Scarlett Neils (7) 146
Terrene Harris (10) 147
Daisy Bradford (7) 148
Brandon Joseph Gaughan (9) 149
Abdullah Mahmood (10) 150
Rhys Kristiansen (8) 151
Reinhardt Aiden Ferrer (6) 152
Thomas Kilpatrick (10) 153

The Poems

Summertime Poem

Ay, hey, hooray!
It's the summer holiday!
Let's play all day!
What would you say?

Let's have fun
In the great shining sun!
Put on the suncream
And lick the ice cream!

Let's kick the football
And don't miss the goal!
Splash in the warm sea,
Don't get stung by the bee!

Jump in the pool,
You don't need to go to school!
The best season of the year,
Every child knows it's here:
Summer!

Flowers, butterfly and bees
Ice cream, beach, shells and the seas
Birthday parties, games and pool
Fun is over - back to school.

Elizabete Ivanova (8)

My Summer Holiday

Let me tell you one of my tales,
About my summer holiday in Wales,
Luckily it didn't hail,
But it did rain, so the beach was a complete fail!

At the beach the tide sailed on the sand,
It looked lovely like a dance,
It reached right over to the huge rocks,
And the wet stairs I had to stand on.

We went to the Welsh Mountain Zoo,
It was so much fun, woohoo!
I'm quite sure the animals were playing peekaboo,
This is oh so true.

My favourite animal to see is a rhino,
So grey and grumpy,
I've always wondered how fast can they go.

When I went to the fair,
The spooky funhouse was like a secret lair,
I did it for a dare,
I wasn't scared.

Wales has a lovely summer breeze,
Although there's lots of bees,
They buzz close to you but it's just a tease.

I loved the ice cream too,
With chocolate sauce, a flake and sprinkles,
Yummy, it's like a dream!

Summer is my favourite time,
It's such a delight to go to the beach and fly a kite,
Maybe next time!

Lola Mujungu (8)

Summer

Summer sunshine,
Flowers abloom.
Splashing around,
In a sunny lagoon.

Lying on the beach,
Getting very tanned.
Sea lapping at my feet,
I'm feeling mighty grand.

Licking yummy ice cream,
On hot and sunny days.
Going to the theatre,
To see some funny plays.

Going on holiday,
Having lots of fun.
Sitting in a deckchair
Underneath the sun.

On the ferry home,
Feeling rather glum.
Suddenly we're there,
Now the journey's done.

Driving to a theme park,
The excitement is immense.
We go on every ride,
And see all the events.

Hot and sweaty days,
Passing very fast.
Only a few left,
Enjoy them while they last!

Ella Paterson (9)

Summertime Is Here

It's summer
Let's go have some fun
It's summer
Let's relax in the sun

Put on your shades
And have fun at the beach
Grab your flip-flops
And listen to that speech

Get in the ocean
Feel that breeze
When you get out
Have some cheese

Go on vacation
And get in the pool
Grab a popsicle
And feel cool

Put on your swimsuit
And lick your lolly
Pull up your trunks
And be jolly

Build a sandcastle
Play with a beach ball
Put on your sun lotion
And go to the mall

It's summer
Camp in the woods
It's summer
Feel those good moods.

Rhianna Sunassee (9)

Our Holiday

At the beach, sand and shells galore,
Sun, sea and sand? I couldn't ask for more!
Ice cream and sandcastles are really very cool!
Back to the hotel to swim in the pool!

Theme parks, roller coasters, come on let's go!
A wasp would definitely be my foe!
Aeroplanes, boats and maybe trains,
On my holidays, they are my mains!

Fun in the hotel, let's go explore!
Or maybe down to the seashore!
In the hotel, rooms and fun!
With our holiday, we're nearly done!

Back in the car, it's time to go.
There's traffic? We have to take it slow!
This is taking forever! We'll never get home!
Daddy took us for ice cream (we got foam)!

Time to pack, sad we had to go.
But on the bright side, it's good to be home!
We got a souvenir, a pack of bubbles to blow,
Our family is loving to the bone!

Leah Young (10)

Fun In The Sun

Barbecues are burning,
Daddy is cooking,
The sausages are sizzling,
The cheese is melting upon the burgers.

Summertime is fun,
Surfing is hurting,
Swimming is soothing,
Mummy is sunbathing,
Watching the fun.

Beach balls bouncing,
The waves are crashing,
The sea is getting nearer,
Time is nearly over,
The sun is setting.

Time to go home,
Sleep off the fun,
Get ready,
Do it again,
Have more fun,
In the sun.

Max Lishman-Neilson (10)

Summertime

The best time of the year,
Yay, summertime,
Long hours in the sun, having lots of fun,
Playing with my friends,
Time feels like it never ends.

Going to the park,
Going to the beach,
Days out with my family and lots of ice cream to eat.

The sun is shining brightly above me,
Streets are filled with laughter and happiness,
Birds chirping and children giggling,
The smell of barbecue,
Mmm, so inviting.

No school, not a care in the world, just free to be me,
How I wish summer would stay forever,
But like they say,
All good things have to end.

Alisha Ghogha (10)

Where's My Lilo?

I was building sandcastles on the beach,
when a gust of wind took my lilo out of reach.

I watched it fly high into the sky
splashing down into the Med,
narrowly missing a swimmer's head.

I leapt to my feet and ran into the sea,
to give chase to the lilo escaping from me.

As I swam after it all I could see
was my lilo flipping and flopping
across the deep blue sea.

As I witnessed my lilo getting smaller and smaller,
before I knew it, it was as far out as a trawler.

So, I said, 'Adios my friend, this is the end,
but who knows we might meet again in Southend!'

Michael Sirapob Brown (9)

Summertime Rhymes

In my heart there are certain emotions,
To say that summer is here,
To be more active in my motions,
That my holiday is coming near.
Shrieks of happiness and laughter fill the air,
Flowers sway to the beat.
Summer, the season of joy, I shall declare,
A time where you shouldn't be on a seat.
People passing by with a smile on their face,
A special scent wafting through,
With my shorts on and a T-shirt of love,
As the cows happily say, 'Moo!'

Sneha Bhudia (10)

Summer

School is out
Days are longer
Our hair gets lighter
Lots of time to chill
Summer reading challenges (my favourite)
Happy, upbeat music that makes me dance and sing like a Brazilian carnival
The days getting longer
And the seagulls eat our fish and chips
To me this is the best season of them all.

Heidi Hanson

My Summer Poem

Frozen peas and lollies,
Both things from your freezer.
You won't need your brollies,
But don't get hayfever.

Ice cream cools you down,
In the summer heat.
Dark colours like brown,
Will give you sweaty feet.

Keziah Davies (10)

Summertime Is Fun Time

Summer
Sensational, relaxing
Sweating, tropical, lush
Dreamy summery fun, unforgettable scorching heat
Roasting, sweltering, tanning
Sizzling, ablaze
Sun.

Aimee Hood (10)

Summer In The South, Summer In The Air!

Summer in the South,
Summer in the air,
Summer in the atmosphere,
Summer's everywhere

The sun beaming above the horizon,
Peeking its way to unveil itself,
Giving us a hot day,
For me and my family to celebrate!

Summer in the South,
Summer in the air,
Summer in the atmosphere,
Summer's everywhere

In the distance we hear the sound,
Of the waves rippling to the bay,
The sea calm and gentle,
And just the sight of a tropical paradise coming its way!

Summer in the South,
Summer in the air,
Summer in the atmosphere,
Summer's everywhere

I lick my ice cream,
With the greatest pride,
My stomach filled with goodness,
Cools me down today!

Summer in the South,
Summer in the air,
Summer in the atmosphere,
Summer's everywhere

And all I can imagine is a tropical paradise that everybody dreams of!

Bhavika Mistry (9)

Summer

Summer
Humid, so hot
Boiling, burning, scorching
Getting dehydrated outside
School off

Summer
Fun and frolic
Swimming, cycling, boating
Active, burning calories
Get fit

Summer
Lots to eat, drink
Fizzing, icing, chilling
Slush and cream, lemonade and berries
Making merry

Summer
Holiday time
Relaxing, rejuvenating, refreshing
Roaming along sandy beaches
Great time

Summer
My favourite season
Exciting, thrilling, amazing
Don't go so soon
Stay forever!

Hanuv Garg (9)

The Drip

I'm a drip of water zooming down a craggy hill,
eating up rocks
a tip of bracken wafting above me,

I'm shooting along the weird and wonderful track,
flying by bilberries of deep blue,
cute smooth brown pine cones
and dark green leaves.

Dribbling past people sitting down eating happy ham sandwiches
playing with my friends,
chasing their puppy in and out of the beautiful pink heather bush.

Gradually I make it into the smooth gentle river,
Past coots, ducks, swans and geese
With a kingfisher swooping down to grab the fish around me for its tea.

Finally I arrive at Carsington Water,
A rowing blade slices through my friends,
I hide in the depths

Suddenly I'm sucked into a long pipe
Getting filtered along with a few of my friends!

After a torturing torture I hear my friends pouring into a shiny metal beaker,
I know I'll be next...

I feel myself falling, falling into the deadly stillness of Jamie's stomach.

Jamie Thomas Kitchen

Summer

Hot days always play
Ice cream and suncream
Seas and bees
Grass sways
Holidays and stays
Fun in the sun
Energetic children
Happy people
Beautiful butterflies
Enjoyable theme parks
Exciting festivals
Lovely picnics
Berries and strawberries
Lush meringue
Tasty Pavlova
Divine cakes
Refreshing smoothies
Delicious sausages
T-shirts and shorts
Caps and sun hats
Flip-flops plus sandals
Skirts and jeans
Sunglasses and shades
Trunks and bikinis
Poppies are red
Violets are blue
Daffodils are yellow
And... jasmines are white.

Rutendo Muchechesi (9)

Summer

Minty fresh, blue ice here, vanilla there, chocolate? Where?
Cheesecake, really, that's new, oh my, look, there's brownies too!
Cone or cup, thin or fat, tall or short, what should I do?
Cone or cup, cone or cup, I don't know, I can't choose!

Watermelons are so cool!
They're my favourite of them all!
Think how they'd fit on the summer beach
A melon bikini, that's how far I'll reach!

I want to get an awesome tan,
Sunbathing, yes I should,
But then again, I could get burnt,
Sun lotion's always good.

S unshine on my burning face,
U nder the palm trees on a sun lounger,
M ore ice cream for everyone!
M um is telling me to get off the hot sand,
E veryone is happy in their bikinis with a tan,
R eality is happy, bright and sunny!

I am gold and bright.
I am a season, you see.
I'm friends with the sea.

Lila Roberts (9)

Here Comes Summer

Last day of the dreary school year
Counting down the seconds and...
Ring!
Hello summer
Oh how I missed the barbecues
Though Mum gets angry when sauce gets down my shirt!
My little sister pushing me into the sea
When I'm trying to relax on the golden sandy ground
(You know how sneaky they are)
Going on holiday to France and taking selfies with the Eiffel Tower
And of course eating croissants all day long
Going bowling
(Even though I'm so bad, my little sister beats me)
But saying that I'm not looking forward to
The bees constantly stinging me
(I always check if I've got honey on)
Having to do all the chores
(It's called summer holidays)
Having to watch Peppa Pig
(I don't watch it. It's my sister!)
Sweat dripping everywhere I look
It actually makes me feel nauseous
But I guess the very best thing about the summer holidays is...
That we don't have to go to school

And the worst thing is... we don't get much time off school
If I were prime minister I would let children have five months off school
Don't you agree?

Ini Atinaro (10)

Summer Spirit

Summertime is here,
the brightest season of the year.
Boys and girls come out to play,
dance about in the hot sunlight.

For everything is dull without some light,
it's the perfect season to go out on a family vacation.
Flowers grow and people cast away their coats,
since they don't have to fear that they will catch a cold.

Everyone dancing joyfully, everyone eating ice creams,
corn dogs especially, for who can forget yummy hot dogs.
Quintessential weather for a barbecue.

You never know if you get another chance.
Happy days don't last long so...
Live your life in this season.

Go and have a dip and make a *splish splash splosh*,
in this torrid meteorology you will enjoy a lot.
Make sure you apply suncream or you will get a rash, rash, rash.
I will never forget these cheerful evocations.

As in a few days autumn will take over.
But we must not forget our vow to summer,
which is to not forget that summer is and will be the blazing season.

Anjal Parizad (9)

Summer Senses

The sun glittering on the deep blue sea
The bright butterflies flying all around
The sweet pink cherry blossom gracefully tumbling
The sparkling bubbles around my body when I jump in the chilly pool

Birds singing as the sun sets
The leaves gently rustling side to side in the floaty breeze
The sound of laughter and fun in back gardens
The popping wavy sound of the sea on the beach

The gentle smell of the flowers in the warm breeze
The fresh green crisp smell as the grass is cut
Mummy's sweet, golden perfume
The fiery red strawberry juice which drips down my chin

Delicious, warm, melted chocolate I'd accidentally left in the car!
The hot, lumpy, brown sausages from the BBQ
The smooth then soft, squashy, juicy nectarine
Being free outside till bedtime

The feel of crunchy, gritty sand on the sea shells
My greasy, sparkly skin covered in suncream
The feel of round, furry peaches
The love of my family on holiday.

Eloise C E Matthews (6)

Summer O' Summer

Summer o' summer,
My favourite season,
Why I like you,
There are many reasons!

Squeaking of birds enchants me,
Blossoming flowers surround me,
Sweet smell of pollen freshens me,
Out comes the sun dehydrating me.

Ice cream and slush,
Juice and berries,
Having cold things,
Making merry!

Boating and skating,
Cycling and swimming,
Going to the park,
It's so exciting!

Summer o' summer,
Hope you come again,
And please do stay,
Just the same!

Gavyam Garg (7)

Why I Love Summer

The sun is shining, it's so bright,
I am so happy it's not night.

I play in my paddling pool splashing all around,
I'm giggling with laughter, making so much sound.

The clouds are so white, just like the moon
we went to the park when it was noon.

Bees are dancing from flower to flower,
they work so hard from hour to hour.

The trees are swishing left and right,
the sun is shining, it is so bright!

The birds are high up in the sky,
we look up and see them fly.

Butterflies are fluttering everywhere around,
they are so pretty they don't make a sound.

I skipped happily in the summer sun,
All of my friends are here, it's so much fun.

Emily Ann Thomas (8)

Summer Poem

Ice lollies, everyone jolly, bluebirds singing
Bluebells and buttercups blooming, sound of bees buzzing
I think we should have some lemon ice, it tastes so nice
The stream running down, not a single frown
The swimming pool lying in the hot, hot sun
Everyone playing, people on the run
You know it's summer when there are barbecues
But what is it like in London? I hear you ask
Some people perched over their balconies
The train on the Tube starting to move
Trains rushing past, really, really fast
Taxis in a line until the clock strikes nine
People, people everywhere running up and down the stairs
Yawning in the morning rush
I see a zebra crossing, it's time to go to the zoo
The giraffes almost touching the sun
The monkeys starting to play
As the tigers lay in the shade
The seals starting to bathe and the
Meerkats eat fruit as the owls hoot
I am full of glee because there's so much to see and do
As the sun is beginning to set that's another summer's day.

Serena Oduka (9)

Summertime

School's have closed,
Let's pack for holidays.
Mallorca, Mallorca,
Here we come!
Let's go to the seaside
And have some fun.
I can feel the soft, silky
sand brushing through my toes,
The trees swaying side to side
When the cool air blows.
Refreshing smell of fish and chips
On top of the ice cream
With choco chips.
Some are surfing,
Some are boating.
Sun is mounting,
Kids are playing.
Enough playing,
We are done,
Let's go home
As we've had,
So much fun.

Anika Jain (8)

It's Summertime!

It is yellow
It is big
It shines
It is bright
What is it?
The sun.

It has lots of sand
It has lots of people
The sun shines upon it
It has a sea and people swim in it
What is it?
The beach.

It has swings
It has slides
It has tennis tables
It has trampolines
What is it?
The park.

Ryan Laurent Xavier Ssimbwa (7)

Summertime Rhymes

Summertime, summertime
Is so fun messing around and
Playing around with everyone
Monday morning you will just be yawning
Relaxing with what you have done
Tuesday you will be on the game
Without anyone calling your name
Wednesday will be the day when you go to the park
Listening to the wind glisten
Or hearing the dogs bark
Thursday will be fursday
When you look after your pet
Walking them around
Or taking them to the vet
Friday will be my day
So I'll do what I want
Summer comes, summer goes
What will happen next year?
Who knows?

Tee-Jay Bruce (10)

Summer Cools

Summer is cool
although I miss school.
I feel stronger
as days get longer
I get into funny fights
with all my rights,
my big bro strikes
as I get on his trikes...
Mum talks to her pet plants,
as I stay close and chase her rants.
Dad gets off the sofa and the phone
and gets into fights with his muscle tone
This summer is getting funnier,
as I go crazy with *the BFG* cruiser;
Dream catching is exciting,
even when I'm curled up in bed in thunder and lightning.
Summers are always cool
though I miss my *little BFGs* at school.

Shreelakshmi Raghuvaran (8)

Summer

The grass so green,
The sun so bright,
Life seems good,
No worries in sight.

Families and friends,
Laughter and bliss,
Each moment passes without a miss.

Weekends to holidays,
Memories and laughs,
Good time to remember,
But how long will it last?

The grass soon fades,
Leaves begin to fall,
School replaces fun,
Oh I'll miss it all.

Sadiman Khan (13)

Summer Fun

I love the summer, it is ever so warm.
But sometimes that can brew up a storm

The days are long, the evenings are sunny.
My little brother's covered in ice cream that is runny.

We play in the park, on the swings and the slide.
I start to count, whilst my friends run and hide.

In the summer, the flowers grow tall and the bees fly high.
Taking pollen to their homes in the sky.

Days at the beach, walks in the sand.
I love family time, holding my mum's hand.

As the summer comes to an end,
I think of the fun times that we all spend.

Ella Schofield (10)

Summer Poem

Sunny moments make every moment special
Sheltering under a tree from the heat
Mum let out a big cloud of gas, *poowee!*
A lot more to explore but I don't know where to start
Every little adventure counts
Making new friends
Seeing eye-popping things
Resting in the melting sand
Where to visit next
Delicious food, yum
Buying a cute nippy puppy
The bed switcharoo
Riding away from enemies
My first bike fail, ouch
I never want this holiday to end
Driving away, I wish we could stay.

Ria Elizabeth Sanderson (8)

Summertime

The sun is always
Awake
This is the time to jump in the
Lake
Lots of people stay inside
Lazy
While others are acting
Crazy
The ray of light is so
Bright
People play outside with their
Kites
The beach is such a beautiful
Sight
That is why summertime is a
Delight.

Glory Nwangwu (9)

Summer Is Here

S ummer smells like smoky barbecues making burgers and chips.
U mbrellas are not needed anymore.
M arigolds are blooming in my garden.
M usic is everywhere around the world.
E njoying the fast roller coaster and tumbling around with my friends.
R ainbows in the bright sky.

H ot days mean swimming in the cool pool.
O range Calippo dribbling down my face.
L emonade goes down my throat like ice water.
I can feel soft wet sand between my toes.
D ays go fast but I can still have more fun.
A holiday trip will make you smile.
Y ummy ice cream on hot days.
S hame summer's not here to stay!

Mya Khela (7)

Summer

Summer is one of the greatest seasons
Perhaps I can give you some reasons
You could sunbathe in the sun
Wow... that would be so much fun!
You can splash around in the sunny beach
And see what pebbles you can reach
You can jump around in the pool
Hopefully it's cool!
You can have a nice little jog
There will definitely be no fog
You can go for a long walk
Take a friend for a talk
You can ride on the swing
There's lots of things to do in summer.
Can you think of another?

Maryam Asghar (9)

Things I Like And Things I Don't Like About Summer

I like to see the sun shining yellow and hot
I don't like to see the black, buzzing fly in my face!

I like the sound of suncream squelch squirting in Mummy's hand
I don't like the loud, moaning lawnmower!

I like the lilies' smell of delicious perfume
I don't like the smell of the stinky, rotten bin!

I like the taste of sweet juicy strawberry triangles
I don't like the taste of slimy, green, bumpy, lumpy broccoli!

I like the feel of the sun shining on me like a warm cuddle
I don't like the feel of suncream all over my face and stinging my eyes!

Lisette G J Matthews (5)

The Holiday Verse

Summer is the season
When flowers like to grow
Rainbow gardens bloom
We don't spy any snow

Fast bikes race down hills like thunder
Through the woods and streams they plunder
People have their tiny shorts on
Enjoying summer before it's gone

Trees bow down
Waving in the bright air
Birds fly onto them
They don't really care

The sun is out
Smiling at dark shadows
Dancing across the sky
Chasing the clouds that it follows
As they roll on by

Rabbits have their babies
In their fluffy little beds
Where they think about the summertime
In their cute but ditzy heads

Old roses turn young
As rain water smoothes their red and waspy tongues
Flowers bring the world to life
With the beauty that becomes

People tie their sun-bleached hair
In a tidy knot
To keep them cool and fresh
From the summer's cheeky plot

Beaches like the desert
Salt water spring
Pink and pretty polished skin
The season that does sing.

Kayla Freeman (9)

Summer Craze

Please pass me my shades because I'm so cool
It's time for us to take a dip in the pool!

It's summertime, let's have some fun
There's ice creams for everyone!

We'll barbecue
There's plenty to share, no need to argue, no need to care.

The sun is hot, let's find some shelter
Or slide into the sea on a helter-skelter.

We'll go to the park and play some games
And continue with our awesome summer craze!

Emilija Atkins (10)

Reach For The Summer

In summer we have lots of fun
We play at the beach under the sun
The salty sea tickles my toes
The baffling wind blows my nose

The waves sway back and forth
As I walk bare on the cool sand
The sun shines so bright up in the sky
As I look up far and wide
I see footprints, patterns and trails
As I see it I see mine

I love the sea, the sand, the sun at the seaside
I love all that I need to see.

Emmanuela Opara (7)

Summertime

It's summertime and to keep cool,
We play in my big paddling pool,
Picnic lunches, games outside,
Let's take the campervan for a ride,
Feeding birds and pressing flowers,
Now there are more daylight hours,

Playing at the park,
We can hear the dogs bark,
Dancing on the beaches,
Eating juicy peaches,
Cooking on the BBQ,
Come on Izzy here's some for you.

Isabella Barber (9)

Summer Fun

The summer is fun,
The summer is sun!

We love sun in summer,
We love fun in summer!

Flowers love fun,
Flowers love sun!

The sun loves fun,
The fun loves sun!

Everyone loves summer fun!

Emma Mahata (6)

Summertime

Summer, summer, flowers on fire,
Poems to inspire.
While I listen to the birds singing in my ear,
When I sit in the garden sunbathing,
Going to the park my family and me all play,
the sand, the trees, lollies - a treat before we go home.
Swimming pool fun, *splish splash*,
inflated animals, hoops and balls in the pool
we have them all.
Seaside is also the place to be,
Ice cream, seagulls, boats and rock
the splash of the waves as they stop.
Feeling of freedom and happy family fun,
long summer days, hours of sun,
I love summer fun, fun, fun!

Charlee Elizabeth Wilson (8)

Amiee's Joyful Summer

Kids with ice cream dripping mouths were collecting shiny shells,
donkeys strolling along the sand with beautiful jingling bells.
People splashing in the salty sea, but the splashing is not for me.
Running along the rickety pier, catching a tricky crab for my dearest dad.
My magnificent mum splashing in the silvery sea,
With my brother, sister and me.
Beans are keen because they're green.
The farmers had seen a royal ice cream.
Over the hilltops and far away
To see the popular poppies twice as nice as paradise.
There is lots of joy on the golden sand with an ice cream in my hand.
Climbing in an ancient castle and playing an old time game,
I'm hiding from Mum and Dad until they call my name.
It's time for home after the joy, laughter and fun in the sun.
Now it's time to say goodbye and snuggle up tight and say goodnight.

Amiee Cox (10)

Summer's Delight

The summer's sun is shining bright,
High up in the endless sky.
It gives and shares wonderful light,
And receives smiley children passing by.

The summer season has finally come.
It is time to have fun.
School is over and holidays arrive,
Go to the beach so please drive.
Swim, paddle, have fun all day.
Take shade underneath a tree and swim in the deep blue sea.

Lick ice cream before it melts...
Fast, fast, fast.
Keep cool so apply some potion,
That is the squirty lotion!

Build sandcastles, there's more to do,
Summer's here so waste no more...
Am I giving you a little clue?

Adults resting in their armchairs,
Popping in their mouth a few eclairs!
Tired of lecturing their children,
About sleep, when the sun is up.

The sea is lapping like a tired dog.
The sun is still like a log.
The golden grains on the beach,
Twinkle tiddlywinks each.

Oh no, summer days are over.
They have passed like a bird over Dover
Summer!

Vedika Sandeep (10)

Summer Summer I'll Always Remember

Summer, summer, I'll always remember
All the fun times we've had together
Like that time we went to the funfair
We went on the ride that took us to the air

Summer, summer, I'll always remember
All the fun times we've had together
Like that time we went to the beach
We had loads of fun till we reached

Summer, summer, I'll always remember
All the fun times we've had together
Like that time we went to the park
We went and stayed there till dark

Summer, summer, I'll always remember
All the fun times we've had together
Like that time we had ice cream
My brain froze and I screamed

Summer, summer, I'll always remember
All the fun times we've had together
Like that time we had a water fight outside
Because we were feeling too hot inside

Summer, summer, I'll always remember
All the fun times we've had together
Like that time we rode a bike
After that we took a hike

Summer, summer, I'll always remember
All the fun times we've had together.

Maariyah Daud (10)

Summer Time

Summertime is sunshine,
The smell of flowers too
The sound of children playing,
In the big, fat swimming pool,
Water fights are also cool,
Eating ice creams with no shoes,
Sitting outside while sleeping,
Fields filled with adventures to be found,
Bugs and creatures all around,
Trees to climb and a forest to find,
That's the meaning of friendship tonight,
Friends to play, all the day,
Hanging out or messing about,
That's the choice you make,
Hide-and-seek or doing tag,
Put them together and you have
Hide-and-seek tag!
Oh, what fun!
And just sprinkle a big field with long grass to play in,
Boys play sports for some time,
Girls hang out and watch them fight,
Holidays are also fun,
Going on an aeroplane or in a car,
It does not matter how far!
New countries to find is harder,
But exploring them is fine,
Trampolines are awesome too,
Bouncing, jumping, doing flips,

Oh my!
Summertime is always a big hit!
Happy summer!

Ema Bredova (10)

Untitled

Summer is hot,
There's sun and shade,
In water we wade,
Frogs and bugs,
It's grass to hug,
Eating outside,
There's a big swing ride,
It's dogs and boys,
Lots of noise,
There's hot, sunny sky,
It's summertime,
Summer, summer,
Is almost here,
Time for fun and swimming gear,
Trips to the beach,
So much fun,
Coming with a baseball,
There's games where we run,
Summer, summer,
Is almost here,
Let's give a big cheer,
Summer is here,
Join along,
There's lots of fun,
Be here and be there,

There are frogs, logs and bugs,
Sunshine is shining,
Shining all around,
Summer is here.

Favour Joy Olorunfemi (8)

Summertime

June, July and August, summertime
The ocean waves in rhythm and rhyme
The beach explodes with castles of sand
Never thinking the seagulls will land
But they do!

Statues sunbathe with still smiles
With cold, fragile shells for miles and miles
Pebbles in the back, an aqua-blue
A long summer tale coming true
And they do!

Sun melting ice creams
Taste the dream
Picnics on the beach
The seagulls screech
And steal the food!

The squeaky striped huts
The human rabbit hutch
For you for sale
At a price beyond the pale
And they are!

The sun cools dripping into the sea
Watched by the litter and one lost bee!
Sunburn around handprints and homeward bound
The ice cream and chip-filled woozy crowd
The dreamy beach gone away.

Lucy Mackie (10)

Summertime

S is for the sun shining down below on us and we are happy because we get all nice and warm.
U is for being under the shade as sometimes the sun is too hot and we need to cool down.
M is for the mornings where we wake up and have a smile so big because we are glad it is the summer holidays.
M is for the marvellous days where we play outside, maybe on the beach someday where we can wriggle our toes in the soft warm sand.
E is for entering the shower every day to cool down from the heat outside.
R is for relaxing on the deckchairs whilst wearing your shades, feeling happy because it is summertime - the greatest season of them all.
T is for the time that flies by because you are having such a fun time in the hot summer air.
I is for ice cream so tasty indeed, I would love to have a 99 please, with some chocolate sauce and some rainbow sprinkles, it would definitely make me want some more.
M is for the muggy days so hot that we stay outside all through the day.
E is for the end of spring, turning into the lovely, wonderful, enjoyable, marvellous, spectacular summer that we all cherish and love.

Lina Sahal (10)

My Long, Long Summer

Twinkling seas, a gentle breeze,
A sandy beach and ice cream.
A villa in Spain, on a country lane
Not a sprinkling of rain, or snow.
A cabin in a wood, outside as much as I could,
Climbing higher than I should, but I was only bruised and bumped.
Walking in the hills, swimming in the ghylls,
Having barbecues and grills, in the yawning months of summer.
It fills my heart with happiness to sing our holiday song,
Of what we'll do and where we'll go all the summer long.

Nuala Sankey (9)

Summertime (An Acrostic Poem)

S unny beaches
U gly pollen
M osquito madness
M assive delights
E nemies are forgotten
R ays of light
T ears are gone
I ce melts
M erry months
E verlasting fun.

Jasmine Richards (10)

Solstice Summer

S weltering sun blazing in the sky,
U nderwater where fishes swim by.
M agical surprises for kids.
M ellow ice cream melting in my mouth.
E ffulgent sun dancing around and around,
R osy roses blooming so round!

First in the sky is faint shimmer,
Next in the sky is a glorious glimmer.
The luxurious sun-filled Mother Earth.
A sun sensational summer!
The delicate flowers swaying side to side in the breeze.
People sizzling in the scorching sun,
Sea so humble and loyal like your best friend.

Summer, summer,
Have picnics with your friends,
Summer, summer,
Have sleepovers,
Have midnight feasts!

S easons of fun,
U nforgettable season.
M aking pictures of us so we have memories of us playing in the summer.
M eadows of sparkly flowers,
E xtra daylight in summer!
R elaxing underneath the trees that give us shade and joy for me!

Jahanavee Sandeep (8)

The Living Tale Of Summer

School is out, we are free,
To involve everything in our personality,
So you should know,
Fun's a yes and school's a no,

Staying up late, being absurd,
Forget about being a little nerd,
Breaking the rules, stepping out of line,
Something in schedule for Frankenstein,

What I am saying is control how you are,
Just don't take it way too far,
We must have fun, it's compulsory,
School is out, we are free,

Going on holiday, maybe Rome,
Searching its history on Google Chrome,
In the deep end, in the pool,
Having fun, now that's a rule,

Having ice cream,
The aroma in your dream,
The melting sensation,
Floods the nation,

So there it is, loud and clear,
Maybe I'll tell the tale in another year!

Zain Jamil (9)

Summertime

Down by the seaside,
Sand between our toes
And that ball of fire in the sky.
But I wonder why, oh why, oh why
Isn't it summer every day?

Family barbecues,
Paddling pool,
Butterflies and ladybirds.
Laughter, fun and games
But I wonder why, oh why, oh why
Isn't it summer every day?

Mint double choc chip,
Three scoops high
And that feeling of cold minty feet,
The feeling of the dry ice cream cone
Slipping down your throat,
But I wonder why, oh why, oh why
Isn't it summer every day?

Summertime is nearly over,
Only a few more weeks,
I stare out
To the wonderful summertime sunset,
And wonder why, oh why, oh why
Isn't it summer every day?

Olivia Howell (11)

Super Summer Fun

B aking people's skin, the sun shines in the sapphire-blue sky.
L aziness is personified as your mum and dad become your servants.
A ll hail the almighty August; the holiday god!
Z ooming down the motorway in a sports car, with a cool breeze in my face, the tunes blasting!
I ce cream cones served on the bay, chocolate, vanilla, or mint choc chip, all you could wish for!
N o more mean maths, evil English or cruel computing!
G et yourself tanned - it's time to chillax!

S wimming in a hectic pool, or surfing on the salty, shining sea.
U tterly awesome, no school for six weeks!
N ow it is the time for us kids to get hyper and turn our parents back to the child in them!

Harriet Tracey (10)

My Garden In The Summer

The garden that is dressed up,
All the colours that are fair.
The birds are singing and the trees are dancing,
What wonder it is to be here.

The garden I can see, that glares back at me,
I wish I could be there.
The water that falls continuously like the purest thing,
The flowers are jewels, and their scent is like lovely perfume.

The bees are busy chatting away, on another sunny day.
The butterflies are as pretty as pearls that glitter,
Oh what joy it is to see such things,
But if only they could be better.

The leaves that silently whisper as the day just goes by quicker and quicker.
The coloured birds all sitting on the dancing trees, how lovely they look.
And now the time has come to pack up,
All the birds fly away,
So do the bees and butterflies,
As now it is night.

The flowers lie down,
And the leaves are quiet, and soon everybody is gone,
Some sleep, some stay awake,
But this is just how life goes on!

Sarah Faraz (10)

Greetings Of Summer

Summer!
Summer!
The most glorious season of all
Last year my cousins came from Canada
To see us all
The sun was shining as bright as stars
And there was joy in our hearts.
The sun makes us smart
The summer was the best
My cousins and I went on a quest
We went to places in the sun
We had lots of fun
The heat felt like fire
It burnt our skin like sapphire
We went to the beach
To the sandy shore
While we were eating we heard the waves roar!
We swam in the waves of the salty sea
As the water came rushing like an angry bee
It was soon the last day
It went so quick and so fast
My cousins then left with a moan and a gasp
There was no time to complain
As autumn was around the corner
So we had to watch out
There was going to be some rain!

Vishaagan Vanigasooriar (8)

Summer Adventures

The summer starts
When I went to France
We went camping in L'Atlantique
If you are going to eat - say: 'bon appetit'!
After France came England
Just so we can get ready for Poland
Polish Airlines are the best
They will take you to your nest
The food was yummy and we flew high
And landed on the farm like a stork from the sky
We loved the dogs, cats and chicken
Not so much the mosquitoes as we've got bitten
We were jumping on the hay
And I fall down so many times I can't even say!
Barbecues were great with sausages sizzling
And spooky games at night
That made us all scream
Magical Gardens - that's not part of the farm
A real fairytale land that gives you lots of fun
Now we are off to Slovakia
Another country on the list
We will meet another grandma
And eat lots of cheese!
Next will be our England - we will go there on the plane
We had a lot of sunshine - let's hope it doesn't rain!

Gabriela Kalinowska (8)

Summer Holidays

Six weeks of holiday,
Lots of things to do.
Mummy doesn't have leaves,
I don't know what to do.

LegoLand is nice
Barracuda is good
Holiday club is boring
I miss my friends too...

Sithija Kurukulasuriya (5)

Summer Days

Great weather, great summer
Summer morning, summer noon
Blossoming flowers, and summery stalks
Summer feels like a great balloon.

Itchy fleas and angry wasps
Bug bumbles like bumbling bees
Ice cream and rainbow lollies
Nicer than ever, as I hear that merry tune.

Plants sprouting with puffy, puffy leaves
Grass swaying in the light soft wind
Blue clear skies and best of all, the bright
Blessed sunshine that shines all around.

The dry earth that actually I quite like,
The fields and meadows so beautiful.
The garden centre, filled with silky green vegetables and summer herbs
Ready to be made into salad, mixed with cream for dinner.

Special cool meals that give summer that great taste
Cool on one side, hot on the other
Full and tired now; but still quite sunny
That's the end of my summer day.

Michelle Oreoluwa Alalade (6)

Summer For Me!

Some might like barbecues in summer,
But not for me!
I like the tickly sand and the blue sky,
And the waves crashing out at sea!

Yes, you guessed it: I'm a beach fan,
With the sand and sea.
I love the fresh air,
And the buzz of a bumblebee!

Making sandcastles and playing jump wave,
And eating hot dogs too!
We mustn't forget candyfloss,
These days are my favourites, I don't know about you!

Next, the funfair awaits us,
Roller coasters going up and down.
And there's also an amusement park,
Flashing and blaring, what a sound!

Finally, our summer day is over,
But we'll be back for more!
It might be end of the day, but not the end of summer,
The beach I adore!

Yusairah Syed (9)

In The Summer

In the summer
Flowers bloom brightly like the sun
In the summer
In the summer

In the summer
You see people swimming and splashing in the pool
In the summer
In the summer

In the summer
You smell freshly cooked sausages on a barbecue
In the summer
In the summer

In the summer
You see lots of people having lots of fun on the beach
In the summer
In the summer

In the summer
You see the sun shining brightly
In the summer
In the summer.

Emily Chambers (7)

My Perfect Holiday

We went on a train
Not too far away
And I have had
The perfect holiday

We got tanned by the sun
And laid down on the sand
We walked by the sea edge
Hand in hand

We went to the beach
With my cousin and aunt
And while we were there
We bought a nice plant

We had a great time
Splashing in the sea
Just my two sisters
My cousin and me

My holiday has been simple
As simple as can be
But that's satisfying enough
For me.

Beatrice Isted-Aggrey (8)

My Summertime Rhyme

Summertime
Oh what a ball
Bugs everywhere
Big and small
Lawnmowers howling
Day and night
Crazy old neighbours
Give me a fright
Water fights soothe me,
When it's hot
Ice-cold paddling pools
For me to spot
Pump action water pistols
To soak my poor mum
Roll over laughing
In the sun
I love the summer
I hate the rain
I feel the cold
In my little frame
So let's run around
Like crazy little monsters
The summertime, always makes me bonkers.

Jack Freeman (8)

A Day At The Beach...

Waves licking ferociously at our feet,
Where the sand and sea will meet,
Sand sticking to the suncream plastered everywhere,
Toddlers naked, they just don't care,
Suntanned bodies dotted around,
Cool! A ten pound note has been found,
Ice cream dripping down the cone,
A small, little sailing boat, out on its own,
Seaside food - never been better,
Fish and chips for me, it's the perfect weather,
Seagulls squawking overhead,
Whilst children feed them crusts of their bread,
Skimming rocks into the sea,
Babies giggling happily,
Fairground music surrounding the beach,
The teddy in the arcade was not reached,
The clinking of the 2p coins being dropped,
Fish thrown back to sea; with a plop,
Sitting on the cob with a fishing line,
'Do we have to go home?' the kids will whine,
Everyone's had the best ever day,
'Of course we'll come back,' the adults will say.

Faith Schooley (12)

My Summer Fun At The Water World

Being excited and bored,
because of waiting in a very long queue for the colourful water slide.
It was a hot and sunny day,
so I couldn't wait for a really quick water slide to get the giant splash.
Sliding down the colourful slide was the best thing to do in the summer.
Swimming in the Water World pool was a pleasure,
it felt like I was a happy mermaid finding a treasure.
That was my amazing memory in this summer.

Rachael Ruixi Chen (8)

Beautiful Summer

Summer means the world to me
It's time for me to relax and lay down
No time to complain and no time to frown
Little children move to the beat
While others prefer sandcastles as a treat
Mothers sunbathing in the heat
While some of the men like cooking meat
While other men like surfing with the waves
Loads of seagulls flying about, even when there is no food to crave
Maybe I'll go camping or build a lemonade stand
Or try and build something grand,
Maybe I'll paint pictures or go to the zoo
Or imagine the sky the colour blue
Eat a cheeseburger or have a picnic at the park
And watch all the tiny dogs bark and stay away from any sharks
It's like this day will never end,
I like camping, exploring too
From the good things to the bad
When the bees sting to when the trees start swinging,
Hiding from the shade
Sometimes summer is annoying and you have to cover your eyes.

Toyin Sarah Joseph (10)

Summertime Rhymes

I like summertime because it's fun,
Eating cheese and a Jamaican bun.

I like summertime because it's hot,
Even though I feel as if I'm in a steaming pot.

I like summertime because I get to play,
Even though it gets tiring every day.

I like summertime because I get to go out,
Even though I'm serious and I don't like to mess about.

I like summertime because it's nice,
Eating chicken with white rice.

I like summertime because it's loud,
Even though I'm not the type to hang with a crowd.

I like summertime because I get to see my family and friends,
And in summertime the fun never ends.

Jayden Roberts (10)

Summertime

Summer, summer, summer, summer
Most of the time you're such a bummer

Summer, summer, summer, summer
But why can't you be a bit more calmer?

Sometimes you're good and sometimes you're bad
But all your sun's shimmer makes me glad

Your sun is shining out and about
But when it's too hot it causes a drought

Spending the day on the stony beach
But sadly the clothes have to go to the bleach

The flowers bloom
But summer ends soon

Goodbye summer, hello autumn
Let the leaves fall and sunshine be forgotten.

Zara Zeynal (9)

Summer In The Maldives

Summer breeze, hot warmth against my skin
And nobody telling me what to do

Play, play and play
Ice cream every day

A small island, a small wonder
Tucked away neatly - a beautiful creation

Silky aquamarine and topaz waters
Serene and tranquil
Surround us as we sleep above

Snorkelling and swimming
Eating and playing
Canoeing and paddling

One day left in this paradise
I will miss it
Until next time my friend.

Syed Ali Tahir (10)

My Summer

I love to go swimming in the pool,
Especially when it's hot, it's so, so cool,
I'm not meant to dive, that's the rule,
The good thing is I'm out of school.

Barbecues are so much fun,
When we eat chicken in a bun,
When I am in the sun,
I just really love to run.

Hayfever is so much pain,
Thank you it's starting to rain,
I would love to visit Spain,
But I'd rather take the train.

Summertime is meant for sharing,
That's why we are always caring.
I love to play in the sun,
But summer is almost done.

Amoya Mullings (9)

On The Beach On A Hot Summer's Day

I stroll across the smooth sandy beach
while eating a perfect peach
I sit under a shady palm tree
As the breeze shifts in the cooling shade
I sit on my knees looking at the bees
Wondering if I was a bee
How cool that would be!
Me and Lee watch the sea
While the sun dances in the reflection.

I dig into my fresh ice cream
Then I eat the ice cream cone
Till it's all gone
It's the time to ignore your phone
Until the sun has gone
Summer is the time to have fun
So don't moan
Talk in a good tone
And go outside to enjoy the sun.

Alima Khanum (12)

My Precious Summer

M y mum took me shopping after I finally did some 11+,
Y esterday I helped her with the cooking.

P reparing for school, I packed my bag with lovely new stationary,
R elaxing in the garden on the sun lounger,
E ating ice cream and cake with cooling milkshakes,
C onvincing Mum to take us to the park,
I rritating sister takes my stuff when I'm not looking,
O beying my mummy's instructions not to hit them,
U sing all my energy on the bike and play,
S ummer is here, my favourite season.

S izzling hot sun in my eyes,
U nique is what I am,
M unching on a bag of crisps while I'm sunbathing,
M e and my three sisters playing all day long,
E ating my favourite food,
R elaxing and playing is what I love, how I wish summer never ends!

Tarneen Kaur Gura (9)

Eva's Summery Poem

Summer's ice cream,
Eat it quick,
Eat it fast
Otherwise it might not last.

Summer's very hot
So don't wear a lot.

Summer is barbecue time
In the garden
All the people looking fine.

Summer evenings are so great
We get to stay up late.

Summer is special,
Summer is sweet,
So listen to my beat.

Eva Smith (6)

My Summer Holidays

The summer holidays have finally come,
When all the schoolwork is done,
Finally I'm free for a run and lots of splendid fun.

Relaxing in the super hot summer sun,
Eating lots of current buns,
Whilst thinking up lots of puns.

Going to the beach,
Hoping to see an ark,
But afraid I might get bitten by a shark,
Suddenly I hear a bark.

My mum's in quite a rage,
I'm so worried I might get locked in a cage,
I've turned the colour beige.
Now I wish I hadn't touched the sage.

Jasmeen Kaur Gura (10)

Holiday Poem!

Camping in Jubilee,
What a nice place to be.
Going to the outdoor cinema,
Watching 'Secret Life of Pets'.
Going to the water park,
Splashing and playing all day long.

Camping in Pickering,
Where are we?
Go Ape, climbing in the trees,
Going out for tea at The Buck.
Falling off the monkey bars, ouch!

Going to Whitby, look at that beach,
On a steam train, there and back.
Mint choc chip ice cream, yum,
Getting splashed by waves, watch out!

Charlotte Rose Heppenstall (8)

Summer Poem

Summer is great
Come on there is no time to waste
There is always a new taste with what you make
It may be a cake or just a Flake

Summer is great
Come on there is no time to wait
You get to skate
Make new friends at the lake
No need to rake
Come on let's celebrate

The sky is blue
No matter what you do cos it is fun
I bet you a ton that life is more fun
Cos the sun is always out.

Joshua Skidmore (9)

Summer

Summer is fun
Summer is hot
Summer is bright
Summer is a walk in the park.

Summer is too hot at times
Summer is too creepy at times with all the insects flying around.

Summer is a time to spend with family
Summer is a time to enjoy.

Summer is too hot at night
Summer is sticky at times.

Summer, summer I will enjoy
as I spend time with my family.

Humairah Banu Akhter (6)

Haven Is The Best

Haven is the best
Get ready for your quest
Come and get a tan
Don't forget a fan
Have fun in the club
While your parents are in the pub
Come to Skegness
The big rides are best
There was a climbing wall
I thought I was going to fall
My legs were like jelly
I had butterflies in my belly
I climbed to the top
But I didn't stop
So have a lot of fun
And play in the sun.

Skye Jessie Hill (9)

Summer's Here!

School has finished
Summer's begun
Me and my family
A summer of fun.

The sun is out
The clouds are in retreat
Sunscreen all over
From my head to my feet.

Relatives from all over
Come to visit
And our time together
Is exquisite.

Hope you have a great summer!

Aasiyah Shajira (9)

In The Heat Of Summer

I can make the colours of a rainbow from the garden hose.
Colours as bright as my shiny clothes.
T-shirt and shorts, that's all I need in this heat.
Even if I get wet it will not be for long.
Catch me if you can, I am full of energy and happiness.
Smiles as wide as the morning sun.

Chijioke Nathaniel Ibeanu (8)

Summer's Here!

S ummer, it's finally here!
U nder the shade, brrr! Nice and cool
M errily jumping about on the beach
M ore, more, more! I want more waves!
E ating lots of ice cream, mmm... delicious
R adiating sun beaming down on my face.

Paula Ampaw-Obeng (10)

Summer

S ummertime is when you eat a bun,
U nder the sun, having lots of fun,
M eeting family and friends,
M ore fun, no need for pens,
E xcited for the next day,
R elax and pray!

Hafsah Mahmood (9)

Summer

S unny summer days
U mbrellas in case it rains
M ud pie by the river
M uddy puddles make you shiver
E vergreen trees shimmer in the sun
R ainy days are never fun.

Lexie Witcher (8)

Summer Holidays!

S is for summer when you have fun,
U is for under the hot, hot sun.
M is for money you spend on your holidays,
M is for more money you spend in the arcade!
E is for extra time spent in bed,
R is for rock pools where you catch crabs in a net.

H is for holidays when you stay away,
O is for outside where you splash and play.
L is for lollies that are very sweet,
I is for ice cream that's a nice treat!
D is for days that are hot and sunny,
A is for ants that eat your dropped lolly.
Y is for yay when it's time for school to part,
S is for summer, now we're back to the start!

Poppy Bradford (9)

Summertime Rhymes

The memorable ebullient days are what ping into my head every second!
I love it when friends come round for a summer adventure.
To enjoy summertime with me and have a great laugh!
The whiff of rightly toasted chicken on the barbecue, drifting through my nostrils.

Every weekend is a rush for Mum,
Always going shopping and getting me new summer clothes to wear.
On the way *ding, ding, ding*, the ice cream van rings!
So many to choose from, which should I take?
In the end we will be worn out!
After a glorious day filled with thrill!

Nearly time to go to bed,
So get a good night's sleep for tomorrow's adventure.
What will it be next?

Swasthika Arunkumar (10)

Summer Holidays

S o much fun
U nderneath the sun
M elting ice cream, lick, lick, lick
M any children playing, quick, quick, quick!
E ating ice creams all day long
R eady to play? So come along!

H aving so much time to play
O ver this happy holiday!
L ovely weather
I n the heather
D oing what I like
A nd riding on my bike
Y ay! I've ridden 'round this bend
S ummer holidays, please don't end!

Ella Plumb (10)

Summer

Tennis - rallies with the coaches,
Back and forth, back and forth...

Violin - pinch and play to make it sound deeper,
Playing on the 'a' string, ringing sound...

Swimming - in the sea, cool on a hot summer's day,
Standing on the bodyboard, wave lifted me backwards,
Jellyfish in the water.

Yurt trip - stick collecting from an ancient wood,
Daddy snapping the branches,
Staying up late and having marshmallows on the fire!

Imogen Lewis (7)

The Sun Is Shining

The sun is shining
The sky is blue
The butterflies are fluttering
The kids are excited for the barbecue

The sun is shining
The sky is blue
The summer air is blowing
The time when you'll never get the flu

The sun is shining
The sky is blue
The sand is sparkling
The summer birds are singing,
Toot, toot too.

Anusha Shams (8)

It's All About Summer

Summer is fun!
For everyone.
Hearing the waves
As you sunbathe.
The deep blue sea
Is for you and I.
The golden sand
And the summer band.
Seagulls flying in the air,
Children playing everywhere.
It's all about summer.
I love summer
The radiance of the sun makes
me smile, it makes me laugh
I love summer.

Amalya-Lovett Akua Antwi-Agyei (9)

Summer

Sun shines
Happy times
Trees grow
Blossoms you know

We love the sun
It brings such fun
To the park, have a run
Ice cream for everyone
Playing games out in the sun

Summer smiles
Greatest days
Friends forever
I wish the summer could stay!

Klyo Anerobi-Mcpherson (8)

My Summertime

School is out, give a shout and cheer,
Let's have some fun, the summer holidays are finally here!
Swimming in the turquoise ocean, under the water we go,
With dolphins swimming in symphony, a couple of metres in front of me.
Swinging on the swings, up and up we go,
Swinging with my friends,
The fun never ends.
Nice refreshing ice creams, let's give a scream,
But it's getting hotter, how about suncream?
The bright yellow, sparkling sun, shining on the sand,
Now doesn't that sound grand.
But now it's time to go home.
Summer's out, school's in
But not to worry, because it's still scorching.

Ocean Tallulah Walton (10)

My Best Summer Ever

S un and fantastic shopping trips
U nhappy when my tooth fell out (ouch)
M am was funny on our days out
M y family and I are so fantastic
E ating my picnic at Allonby beach
R ain ruining our plans

H appy when I went to Fairy World
O ur family are great
L ove my family with lots of love
I love spending time with my dad
D ad is so funny and joyful
A day in summer makes me happy
Y ou are the best family ever.

Paris Kia Cookson (10)

Fizz-Whizzing Summer Goals

S unbathing on your towel while you're getting a
gorgeous, great, golden, sun-kissed tan
U nderneath the beautiful, bright, blessed, luxurious sun
M aking nutritious, nourishing, natural, finger-licking food
M ost certainly not forgetting to put enough excellent,
elegant sunscreen on for health reasons
E ating and drinking sufficient, suitable, surplus, refreshing
food (watermelon, lemonade etc)
R eally enjoying the relaxing, cheery riot and joining in the
enjoyable festive fun.

Dana Farajallah (9)

Summer

Spring has ended
It's summer now, I can't wait to have fun
It's now where smiles spread
I can't wait to jump in the pool
I am never dull or angry, just happy, happy, happy
Oh lovely and bright summer is
I am just starting
So why aren't you eager to read more?
There are more things to do
In one word, it is fun
But it all ends in one place
You only hear and see the birds tweeting with sadness
And the flower petals falling
Down, down, down!

Megha Sheby (9)

Happy Days

Happy days in the summer
Playing games with one another
Making happy memories
With friends and families

Happy days in the summer
Days just getting funnier
Making new friendships with friends
Hoping that the friends will never end

Happy days in the summer
And at the end of the day sitting by the campfire
And cooking foods with so much joy
Then dancing and singing with each girl and boy.

Harriet Rose Kemeny (10)

Summer

Summer comes once a year,
A happy time this is,
All the children give a cheer,
Holidays are here.

The sun rises bright in the morn,
The flowers are beautiful and smelly,
The fields are looking yellow with corn,
The gardens are green with the lawn.

I love this holiday time,
When I play or sleep when I want,
I can swim, I can dance, I can climb
And the weather can be bright and fine.

Paul Beard (8)

Summertime

Swimming in the pool
Rainbows are cool
No more school
Summertime

Going outside
Going on a fun ride
Get your hair dyed
Summertime

Always sleeping in
Throw working in the bin
Never drop a pin
Summertime.

Poppy Reeves (10)

In The Summer

I cy drinks to keep me cool
N obody wants to stay indoors and be a fool

T he sun shines brightly on my skin
H eating up all the rooms and now we are all doomed
E ating salad, wishing we could win this ballad

S wimming in the cool water, sunbathing
U nderneath the cool breeze
M elting ice creams dripping down to my knees
M um's got a tan and I need a fan
E veryone gets together and has a blast
R ough stones on the beach against my wet feet.

Umar Francesco Kunateh (6)

Our Trip Of Danger

In rafting you paddle along
A river with an oar
And get orders from the guide.
You get wet by the currents of water
And the boat jumps up and down.
There was a fresh water spring
So we stopped to have a drink
The guide told us that people
From the hills come to collect this water.
There were lots of waves
And I almost fell in
It was a fun and dangerous activity
But thankfully nobody did fall in.

Aleš Kilpatrick (7)

Summer Is Here

Summer is here
Sun is fun
Sports day, time to run
Sit outside in the sun
Summer has come
Winter is gone
Competitions have begun
I play out with my kite
That is bright in the sunlight
It's very fun
In the sun
To have lots of fun
As summer doesn't last long.

Aamna Begum (6)

Summer - Tanka

Summer is great fun
When farmers harvest their crops
Children laugh and sing
People go on holiday
The sun is extremely hot.

Matthew Munson (8)

Summer's Here!

S un shining through beautiful windows,
U nder trees is where we keep safe from sun rays,
M eeting family and going on holiday,
M aking friends and playing together,
E veryone having fun, it's all they ever wanted,
R ipe fruit juice leaving an explosion of flavours in your mouth,
S wimming in the outdoor pools,

H otels full of happy families,
E xtra long days to enjoy even more,
R ides are running at the fair,
E njoy it whilst it lasts 'cause summer doesn't last long.

Madison Keiley Elliott (9)

The Seaside

At the seaside, what do I see?
I see the pine wood pier
As the waves crash against it.
At the seaside, what do I hear?
I hear the squawking seagulls
Calling to each other in the sky.
At the seaside, what do I taste?
I taste the salty sea while I'm swimming.
At the seaside, what do I smell?
I smell inviting ice cream.
At the seaside, what do I feel?
I feel the crumbling sand on my toes.

Honey Edwards (7)

My Summer

Sometimes summer
Can be a bummer,
Unless I go to Disneyland Paris
Bonjour!
Or maybe I could go to Thorpe Park
Rather than climbing up a tree bark.
Probably I could go to Weston-super-Mare
And also the fair,
Actually I should go to Legoland
Or maybe form a band.
This is my summer
Hope yours isn't a bummer!

Aleema Mirza Hamid (9)

Summer's Sensations

Sweet, luscious scented roses fill the air,
Whilst watching cute offspring prance with Mother Hare,
Then when evening strikes, the barbecue lights,
But before then, you have to run right, flying the kites!
When you go into the sea, make a splash,
You topple down, making a mighty great crash!
Before going back to your beach hut to have tea,
One last dip in the bright blue sea,
Then at the end of a day at the sea,
The best thing about summer is...
Afternoon tea!

Isabel Amelia Arrowsmith (10)

Summertime

It's summertime, time for a rhyme,
Time to have lemonade with lime,
I've been for a climb
And the weather is sublime.
I can't wait to reach the beach
To feel the sand beneath my feet
I feel the heat and eat lots of sweets
This is such a treat
We're all having fun in the sun
Running away from bees hiding behind trees
I think you all agree, life is fantastic when it's 28 degrees!

Keira Ureta (7)

Picnic

I want to go to a picnic in the summer,
I could play bat and ball with my brother.

The blanket would be green and blue,
And I could fly my kite too.

I tow my boat and sail,
Then go for a ride on my bike, making a trail.

I love summer!
I'd love a picnic with my mother and my baby brother.

Layla Zewin (7)

Summertime Fun!

Bees are buzzing,
Pollen is fizzing,
Summer goes,
The boat rows,
A flying bird,
People heard,
Passed by,
With a blinded eye,
Oh how I love summer,
With the smell of barbecues,
And the sight of people in the swimming pools.

Zara Ahmad (8)

Summertime

S ummer smells like lovely, crispy, pure sea air
U nhappy is not how we feel
M um cooks beautiful meals that taste like fresh berries
M eeting friends at the beach sounds like the noise of magical waves
E veryone looks like they are having fun
R elaxing on a sun lounger feels like heaven
T ime ticks by and sounds like birds tweeting and chirping
I ce cream tastes like creamy and glossy drops of sunshine
M aking noises of laughter in the garden as the smell of a barbecue smokes away
E ndless days look like pure blue sky gleaming down on people.

Ross Jefferies (9)

Summertime

When spring ends, we say hello to summer.
Summer is the season you're meant to be in,
It is a time that will make you feel awesome.
Watching the blazing sunshine fill the day with happiness,
And feeling the wind gently brushing past us
As if it is giving us a tender kiss.
So maybe you're sunbathing in your garden or perhaps the beach.
But as the sun sets there is a new day to wait for.
No matter if it is sunshine or rain
When good things end better things begin.

Jitong Yi (11)

Summer Fun

S unset, sunrise. The sun takes up the whole of the sky.
U mbrellas dancing in the summer showers.
M ake memories whilst having fun.
M unch on food, eat a ton of ice cream.
E njoy the holidays, it's your chance to be free.
R un around whilst you are young.

F eel the sand brush against your feet.
U nder the waves of the sparkling sea.
N ow, it's only just begun.

Hadiyh Roostaei (10)

Summertime Poem

Summer is bright, summer is fun.
Mountains of happiness for everyone.
Holidays, happy days, everyday joys.
Sometimes frustrated by the noisy boys.
Tennis, badminton, what are you going to do?
I love tennis, thank you.
Ice cream, burgers, what a lovely dinner!
Looks like we're going to get no thinner.
Let's go down for a picnic in the park.
It doesn't look like it's going to rain like in Noah's ark.

Kerensa Meredith Lawrence (6)

Summer Holidays

The summer holidays are as good as tea,
It's like having a swim in the sea.
In the summer holidays I went to the swimming pool
And then I felt cool.
In the summer holidays I went out to play.
Once I got so happy that I had nothing to say.
In the summer holidays I went to the ice cream van,
Later on I went to the store to get a Coke can.
Every year I go to a theme park,
Time flies by like a speeding shark.

Raihan Rahman

Summertime

S wimming in the sparkling sea,
U nder the seaweed we slide,
M ischief is made on the beach,
M y ice cream has melted - it's so hot,
E verybody cheer, the holidays are here,
R ound the roundabout we go,
T rain goes crazy - *choo choo*,
I 'm whizzing down the slide,
M y turn again, let's go,
E veryone having fun in the sun.

Aubrey Walton (8)

I Love Summer

I love summer a lot, a lot,
I love summer because it is hot,
I love summer, we have ice cream,
I love summer, the grass is green,
I love summer because we go on a plane,
I love summer and we can go on a train,
I love summer, we go on holiday,
I love summer, we can go out to play,
I love summer because it is fun,
I love summer with everyone!

Luca Scanlon (7)

What I Think About In The Summer

It used to be a bud,
But now it's not,
It's a spiky leaf upon a purple thistle,
I wonder why the petals are noticed but the leaf is not,
Equal as they grow together in fresh spring,
Seen on a blazing summer's day,
Leaving in the windy autumn,
Gone in the snowy winter,
So why is the leaf never noticed?
I will never know...

Misba Khan (9)

My Holiday

I like swimming in the pool on the sunny, funny days.
I enjoyed being in the castle, it was a fantastic place.
I love drawing flowers and I like running with my bare feet.
I fancy eating ice creams because they are sweet.
I like when the birds tweet and I have someone new to meet.
I hate having accidents and going to the hospital.
I don't like it when it's raining on my meal.
I don't like when the holidays finish
Because I have to go to school and learn more English.

Pola Szczygielek (6)

Beautiful Summer

I love summer because of many things!
C reamy and cold ice cream, yum!
E njoying the funfairs and parks!

C olourful flowers blooming everywhere!
R abbits hopping around on the lovely green grass!
E veryone loves going to the beach!
A re you enjoying summer?
M any flavours of ice cream to enjoy!

Umaima Ayaz (9)

Summer Delight

I n summer days when outside's hot
C an't stop, play and sweat a lot
E very kid, babies or scholars

C reamy thoughts, delicious colours
R un all at once to meet the man
E asy comes with singing van
A pple, chocolate, berry flavours
M elting, cold, everyone favours.

Ovidiu Baraban (8)

Holidays

H olidays are my best time of the year
O h, how I wish summer could last forever!
L ovely flowers in the park of multi colours
I ce cream I can eat all day...
D ays are long, nights are short
A lways I'll go to the beach to make sandcastles
Y ou will always see me jump for joy
S ummer is here and I am having fun.

Luca Nocerino (7)

Untitled

Summer, summer, summer.
Ice lollies and ice creams dripping down to the ground.
Barbecue smells enter my nose,
All the flowers blossom out to pose.
Summer, summer, summer.
The sound of the beach, waves roar swiftly across the land,
The food making people wander into restaurants.
Summer, summer, summer.

Hamza Ahmad (11)

Summer

Finally it has come, the summer!
Sunny days like no other
No more work, no more teachers, just play!
And for a whole month, hooray!
If you like ice cream and you like everything nice,
Then you should listen to my advice,
Summer is the best time of the year,
Everyone knows that!

Rishabh Murali (8)

Summer Sunshine

Summer sunshine in the park,
Giggling and laughing till it's dark.
Roses red and flowers bloom,
No more sitting in the gloom.
Grass tickling my toes
And my big fluffy dog licking my nose.
Things like those to always remember,
Before going back to school in September.

Annabel Lucy Bulley (8)

Summertime

A t summertime I eat ice cream
C hill out in a chair and do nothing
R unning in the garden
O r playing under the shade
S un gives you vitamin D
T ime to climb trees
I ce cream for everyone
C ustard also on top, mmm...

Hannah Thomas (7)

Summer Fun

In summertime we play outside,
On our bikes we go for a ride.
We take a picnic to the playpark,
Running, jumping until it gets dark.
To keep us cool we jump into my swimming pool.
We sometimes go in our campervan to Castle Ward,
Where we never ever get bored.

Charlotte Barber (7)

What Summertime Means To Me

The flowers bloom in spring.
Summertime sun helps them grow
And the butterflies flutter by and around the flowers.
The sun glitters on the flowers
And the bees collect pollen from the flowers.
They buzz all day
And make us yummy honey for our tummy.

Alice Emily Bradley (5)

Joys Of Summer - Haiku

The sun is shining
Summer holidays are fun
We go to the beach.

Harry Munson (6)

Summer

S un glinting on the grass, making it shine like emeralds.
U nder the trees we play all day, bursting with energy,
M aking dens to play in, with floors made of ferns.
M illions of butterflies fluttering around us, creating a beautiful sight.
E ating ice cream under the cloudless sky...
R emember, winter's coming - faster than you think.

Emily Walker (9)

Summertime

S ummer is always a delightful time of year
U nder the cool, clear water, relaxing calmly by the seaside
M esmerising fun time
M eaty barbecues at 'Box-Up Crime' club, mmmm...
E verlasting, enjoyable experiences
R eading challenges, so exciting and exhausting under the hot, scorching sun, this is my summertime.

Tyra Sackey (8)

Untitled

P icking out what outfit to wear
I ce cream trucks go by while time flies
C rying children have a tantrum for not getting a prize
N eighbours are joining to eat our delicious apple pies
I nteracting with family and friends
C ome on, take a picture with the new camera lens!

Jenny Yule (9)

Summer

S oaring through the water on a summer's day
U sing all my skills to have a great play
M y diving board is very springy
M y jump is very high
E legantly I dive right to the bottom of the pool
R esults are very good, I came first place in the seven-year-old group!

Harshant Singh Randhawa (7)

Summer

S is for the sun shining in the sky,
U is for the umbrella hardly used,
M is for making the most of the sun,
M is for many days out with my family,
E is for enjoying the holidays,
R is for the return to school at the end.

Ty McCann (10)

Summertime

Summer is a lovely time
When the birds are chirping in the tall green palm trees
And planes are zooming past you
The wavy waves are crashing on the beach
The people are playing in the sea
The whippy ice cream keeps you cool.

Isabelle Wooldridge (6)

Summer

S unshine is great
U mbrellas and rain I hate
M aking sandcastles at the seaside
M y mum made me go on a very fast ride
E ating delicious ice cream
R unning and splashing in the stream.

Emma Hollie Birch (7)

Scarlett's Summer Dream!

S ummer is the best
U nder the trees
M y swimming costume is the best
M y coconut water is delicious
E ggs in summer
R eading under a coconut tree while the sun shines on my feet.

Scarlett Neils (7)

Summer!

S unny and always hot
U nlikely to be cold
M ore happiness
M akes us be joyful
E ncouraging people to come out
R emembering the happy days, when we can all run, jump and shout.

Terrene Harris (10)

Summer

S un shining really bright
U p until almost midnight
M aking lots of memories
M y favourite time of year
E veryone out in the hot, hot sun
R elaxing fun for everyone!

Daisy Bradford (7)

Summer

S melly fertiliser
U nbelievably hot!
M any ice creams to enjoy
M ountains of water bombs to throw!
E veryone loves the summer
R eally, we even love the manure!

Brandon Joseph Gaughan (9)

Summer

S uper water fights in summer
U nderwater swimming cools you down
M ad for ice cream
M elting ice
E ating ice cream
R ed balls are fun.

Abdullah Mahmood (10)

Summer

S unny mostly
U nusual weather
M ight rain so put your hat on
M ust wear suncream
E xciting stuff to do
R un wild in the fields.

Rhys Kristiansen (8)

Summer Holiday

In summer I went to the beach
In summer I went to the swimming pool
In summer I went to the playground
In summer I played in my garden
In summer I went to Kent.

Reinhardt Aiden Ferrer (6)

Tom In The Pond

There once was a boy called Tom
Who one day fell in the pond
He was wearing his hat
Which was grabbed by a bat
Of headwear it must have been fond.

Thomas Kilpatrick (10)

Young Writers Information

We hope you have enjoyed reading this book – and that you will continue to in the coming years.

If you're a young adult who enjoys reading and creative writing, or the parent of an enthusiastic poet or story writer, do visit our website **www.youngwriters.co.uk**. Here you will find free competitions, workshops and games, as well as recommended reads, a poetry glossary and our blog.

If you would like to order further copies of this book, or any of our other titles, then please give us a call or visit **www.youngwriters.co.uk**.

Young Writers
Remus House
Coltsfoot Drive
Peterborough
PE2 9BF
(01733) 890066
info@youngwriters.co.uk